The Discovery Books are prepared

under the educational supervision of

Mary C. Austin, Ed.D.

Reading Specialist and

Lecturer on Education

Harvard University

PROPERTY OF
COMMONWEALTH OF PENNSYLVANIA
ESEA ---- TITLE II ⟶ 1967

A DISCOVERY BOOK

GARRARD PUBLISHING COMPANY
CHAMPAIGN, ILLINOIS

Kit Carson

Pathfinder of the West

by Nardi Reeder Campion

illustrated by Shannon Stirnweis

*For Tom, Tad, Toby, Russell
and Cissa Campion—
without whose help this
book would have been
finished much sooner.*

Copyright 1963 by Nardi Reeder Campion

Manufactured in the United States of America

Library of Congress Catalog Number: 63-9219

6/18/68

92

1356

E S E A   Title II 1967

Contents

Kit Carson: Pathfinder of the West

Chapter *1*

"Merry Christmas, Mrs. Carson"

"Merry Christmas, Mrs. Carson," said Mr. Carson, bending over his wife's pillow. "Thank you for the gift you've brought us this Christmas Eve. December 24, 1809—that's a day to remember."

"Which is it?" asked his wife.

"A boy."

"*Another* boy?"

"Guess you'd like a girl, Becky, but the frontier needs men, and so do the Carsons."

"Let's call him Christopher," said Mrs. Carson. "Christopher Carson. Doesn't that sound important, Lindsay?"

"He looks too small for such a big name. Maybe we'd better shorten it to Kit."

Christopher Carson never grew to fit his long name. His small size always made him very unhappy. Once, when he was eight years old, he overheard his mother and father talking about him. "Lindsay," said his mother, "I wish you wouldn't let little Kit chop down trees. Let the big boys do it. He's too small for that dangerous work."

"Chopping isn't so dangerous, Becky, if you watch out. Kit's the runt of the litter, all right. But out of ten children, one puny one isn't bad."

Kit felt as though his father had hit him in the face. "The runt of the litter?" He didn't weigh much, and his legs were short. But was he a runt? Kit looked into the bit of broken glass the Carsons used for a mirror. He saw a blue-eyed, sandy-haired boy. He saw a face tanned and freckled by the sun. "I may be small," he thought, "but I'm strong. I'll show them."

"Lindsay Carson," Kit's mother was saying, "I don't think you know what the word *danger* means. If you did, we wouldn't have left Kentucky.

Here in Missouri wild animals and Indians are everywhere."

"My folks came over from Scotland 50 years ago, Becky. They weren't looking for safety and comfort. They were pioneers. And that's what we are, Becky, *pioneers*. And danger is our middle name."

Life on the frontier was rugged. The Carson children did not go to school. But they learned the ways of the woods from their father. Kit could not read or write, yet he knew the names of all the trees and how each was used. He knew the habits of the wild animals. He could build clever traps to catch them.

Kit worked hard to make up for his size. He used his eyes and ears.

He noticed all sounds and animal tracks. He taught himself to "freeze." He could hold so still that animals and Indians did not know he was nearby.

Kit was happy in the forest, except for one thing. He did not have a gun. He had to hunt with a bow and arrow. His eyes were keen. He could hit a squirrel on the run with an arrow. But he wanted a gun.

On his birthday, Kit begged his father, "Now that I'm nine, can't I have a gun? I want a flintlock rifle, just like yours."

His father shook his head.

"Why not? I can hit a nail head at 20 feet with your gun."

"Oh, you're a good shot, Kit. I'm proud of that. But we are too poor.

We can't buy another gun. Maybe if we can trap a lot of beaver next spring. . . . Now come along and help me burn trees in the field we're clearing for a corn patch."

Kit's eyes filled with tears. Nobody knew how much he wanted a gun.

All that day Kit and his brother, Big Mose, worked with their father. They chopped trees and cleared land in the cold autumn sunshine. As night fell, they made a roaring brush fire. Lindsay Carson would not stop. He picked up his axe and attacked another tree. Suddenly Kit heard a crack, and then a scream. He turned and saw a big limb crash down on his father. Lindsay Carson fell to the ground.

Kit and his brother ran to him. They could not move the heavy oak branch. "What will we do?" yelled Big Mose. Little Kit bent double and crawled underneath the branch. When he reached his father, he was dead.

That night Kit was sitting by the fire with his head in his hands. Death was common enough on the frontier. But this was different. Kit began to sob. Then he felt a hand on his shoulder. He looked up. His mother was standing beside him. In her hand was his father's flintlock rifle. She held it out to Kit.

"This is your gun now, Christopher," she said. "You're a boy no longer. Today you became a man."

14

Chapter *2*

Oh, To Be a Mountain Man!

"I don't want to be a saddle maker, Mother," said Kit Carson. "I'm going to be a hunter and trapper. I want to live in the forest and be free."

"No, Christopher. You are going to be an apprentice and learn a trade. Hurry now, Mr. Workman is expecting you."

Mr. David Workman's gloomy saddle shop smelled of dust and leather. Its stale air made Kit cough. Mr. Workman scowled. "Just sign the papers please, ma'am," he said.

"What do the papers say?" asked Mrs. Carson.

"That yonder boy is bound out to David Workman, saddler, of Franklin, Missouri, for seven years."

"Seven years!" thought Kit. "I won't last seven weeks in this dust bin. I need air."

Mrs. Carson and Kit each drew an "X" on the paper. Neither one could read nor write.

"Good-by, son," said Mrs. Carson. "Work hard." There were tears in her eyes.

"Do my best, Ma," said Kit. He tried hard to swallow the lump in his throat.

Mr. Workman was a kind man, but he expected a lot of Kit. Kit hated being shut up in the shop, making saddles. Outside he could see the wagon trains getting ready to go West. How he longed to join them!

The mountain men came into the shop to get their saddles and harnesses fixed. Kit listened eagerly to their tales of danger, hunger, blood and sweat. His head hummed with dreams of adventure.

"Boy!" yelled Mr. Workman, "watch what you're doing! That gun cover looks like a pillowcase."

Kit tried to pay attention. Even as a boy, he wanted to do things well.

But Kit Carson's heart was always outdoors with the mountain men. One day he could stand it no longer. After Mr. Workman went to lunch, Kit left the shop. He stopped the first mountain man he saw.

"Mister, don't you need a helper? I'll do anything you ask—anything. Please take me West with you."

The frontiersman looked down at the eager blond boy. Then he laughed. "What do you think we're running? A nursery?"

Kit gasped, "But mister, I'm fifteen."

"You look about ten. So you want to go West? I'll give you some advice. Grow up!"

Kit walked slowly back to the shop. His head hung down. He was miserable.

"Grow up?" he thought. "I'm as big as I'll ever be."

It wasn't until a year later that Kit got his chance. One day, when Mr. Workman was out, a stranger came into the shop. He was dressed in buckskins trimmed with fringe and beads.

"Captain Charles Bent?" asked Kit.

"How'd you know my name?" said the man.

"Everybody knows you, Captain Bent. I guess you're the most famous trader there is."

Captain Bent looked pleased.

"I've been watching you get your wagon train ready, sir. I've counted 28 wagons."

"Right. We start rolling toward Santa Fe in the morning."

"Captain Bent," Kit's heart was pounding so fast he could scarcely talk, "you *must* need an extra hand. Do you, sir? Do you?"

"What about your job here?"

"Oh, Mr. Workman wouldn't miss me. He doesn't think I'm worth anything." This was not quite true, but Kit was desperate.

Charles Bent looked the boy over carefully. There was something about him. "Can you ride?" he asked.

"Yes, sir. Rode before I walked."

"Are you afraid of Indians?"

"No, sir."

"You got a gun?"

"Got my Pa's. And I can shoot it."

Bent rubbed his beard. "I could use another cavvy boy to help on this trip.

The cavvy boys take care of the extra horses, mules and cattle."

"I can do that," said Kit. "I know I can." His eyes were shining.

"I like the look of you, lad. Come 'round to my wagon tonight. I'll get you a mule to ride. We hit the trail at sunup." Bent started toward the door. Then he called back. "Oh, yes. One more thing. I pay cavvy boys a dollar a day."

Captain Bent strode out into the sunlight. Kit sat down and shook his head. A dollar a day! Why, he would have *paid* to go with Captain Bent. That is, he would have, if he had had any money. Captain Charles Bent was a great man. And he had not even mentioned Kit's small size!

Chapter 3

One Cent Reward

Kit pulled his blanket around him. He was tired but he could not sleep. The ground was hard. He ached all over. He sat up and rubbed his back. In the moonlight the white-topped wagons looked like ghostly sailboats.

Yeee-o-o-o-w. A howl came out of the night. Kit shivered. Wolves. He got up and warmed his hands by the campfire.

"It's only sixteen miles back to Franklin," said a voice. Kit whirled around. Behind him stood Captain Bent.

"It's not too late to turn back, lad."

Fear gripped Kit. "Aren't I doing the job right, Captain?"

Bent smiled. "You're doing fine, lad. I watched you. You have spunk."

Captain Bent's words helped Kit. He needed encouragement.

The trip to Santa Fe was long and hard. Soon the food ran low. They had nothing to eat except coffee and salt pork.

Captain Bent sent for Kit. "Lad," he said, "you're a fast rider. Gallop ahead and look for food. We're close to starvation."

Kit was proud to be given such a job. But at the end of the day he returned, discouraged. Across his saddle hung a dead wolf.

"Captain," said Kit, "I'm a failure. All I could find was a pack of wolves."

"Wolves!" cried Bent. "Great! How far away?"

"Just beyond the river. But, Captain, what good are wolves?"

"Oh, you've a lot to learn, lad. Wolves mean buffalo. The wolf pack follows the buffalo herd. They want meat as much as we do. Let's go!"

Captain Bent was a skilled hunter. That night Kit ate roasted buffalo under the stars. Kit ate a lot of buffalo in his lifetime. But it never tasted as good as it did that first night.

At last Bent's wagon train rolled into Santa Fe. Kit liked the Mexican town with its narrow streets and pretty girls. Captain Bent was returning to Missouri.

But Kit had no desire to go back right away. He called on Captain Bent to say good-by.

"Sit down, lad," said Bent. "This Missouri paper just came in by stage-coach. I want to read you one of the ads:

'Notice: Christopher Carson, a boy about 16, small for his age, but thickset and light haired, ran away about September 1st. He was bound to me to learn the saddler's trade. All persons are warned not to hide this runaway. One cent reward will be given to anyone who brings him back.

David Workman
Franklin, Missouri.
October 6, 1826.' "

Kit turned pale.

Captain Bent shook his head sadly. "I'll have to send you back, lad."

Kit doubled up his fists. He felt like crying. Then he looked closely at Captain Bent. The captain's blue eyes were twinkling. The older man threw back his head and laughed.

"One cent reward! Ho! Ho! Ho! Pretty cheap price!"

Kit began to laugh too. "I told you, sir, Mr. Workman didn't think I was worth much."

"Well," said the captain, "I could tell Mr. Workman some news. Kit Carson may be young and he may be small. But he's worth a whole lot. He's the best trail rider I've seen in years."

Kit grinned. He felt eight feet tall.

Chapter *4*

Attack!

After Captain Bent left, Kit did not know where to turn. He couldn't find a job in Santa Fe. A few scouts from Bent's caravan were going to nearby Taos, and Kit joined them. Taos was headquarters for the mountain men. But it was no place for an undersized boy to find work. Soon all of Kit's money was gone.

Then he ran into a piece of good luck. At Ewing Young's Trading Post he saw a man he knew. It was Old Kincade, who had lived near the Carsons in Missouri.

"Well, bless my soul, boy," said Old Kincade, "you got no place to live? Just come right out to my hut."

Old Kincade was poor and sick, but he had been a great hunter. He taught Kit many things. "Now, son," he would say, "you got a good memory. I know that by the easy way you pick up Spanish and Indian talk.

"We got no maps out here, just memory. So you put your memory to work. Never turn a bend in a hurry. Look back and learn the lay of the land. Never leave a river in a hurry.

They're all different. Learn how it tastes and looks and runs. Then you'll know it when you see it again. Keep looking and learning all the time, Kit."

When spring came, poor Kincade died. Kit hit the trail again. He hiked 80 miles back to Santa Fe. He lived on rabbits and prairie dogs. But he still could not find a job. He walked the 80 miles back to Taos. He went straight to Young's Trading Post.

"Captain Young," he pleaded, "please let me work for you."

Young looked Kit over. "You're too small," he said bluntly.

Kit groaned. "That's what they told me in Santa Fe."

Young looked puzzled. "How did you get here from Santa Fe?"

"Walked."

"WALKED? How long did it take?"

"Three days."

"What did you eat?"

"Anything I shot."

There was a long silence. Then Ewing Young spoke again. "You're hired. You're small, but you're tough. I'm heading north with 40 men to trap beaver. We can use you."

"Mr. Young, why is everyone crazy over beaver?" asked Kit.

"All the men back East and in England, too, are wearing high hats made of beaver. It's the style. A trapper can get rich on beaver."

That year Kit learned a lot about trapping beaver. The best time to catch beaver is when the weather is cold.

Then their coats are thickest. But you have to catch them before the streams they live in are frozen over.

Kit learned to spot signs of beaver. Beavers use logs to build houses and dam up streams. A bit of torn bark or a chewed tree told Kit beavers were nearby. He learned that beavers can smell a man a mile away. Only water washes away the smell of man. Kit waded into swift, icy rivers to set the traps. The traps were heavy to carry. They were built to hold a 50 pound beaver when he was fighting mad.

Captain Young taught Kit how to skin a beaver and how to stretch the skin on sticks to dry. He showed him how to roast the body and eat it. Kit even learned to like toasted beaver tail.

The trappers were always in danger from the Indians. One day Young's men were working along the Salt River. Suddenly Ewing Young held up his hand, warning the men to be quiet. They knew what he meant. *Indians!*

"Grab your guns," whispered Young. "Head back to camp. Hide under blankets, packs, anything. Hide!"

Back they ran. Kit crawled under his blanket. He held on to his father's gun. His heart beat fast. This seemed an odd way to fight Indians.

Kit peeped out. The ridge above was covered with Indians. Young and his 40 men were clearly outnumbered.

"We'll all be scalped," thought Kit.

"Hold your fire," whispered Young. "They'll think we've gone."

Kit listened to the Indians coming nearer and nearer. He wished Captain Young would let them shoot. Now the Indians were right in the camp. Then Young shouted, "FIRE!"

BANG! BANG — BANG!! BANG!!!!! YIP—EEE!!!!

Indians dropped on every side. Those who could, turned and ran. Some of Young's men chased them.

When the attack was over, fifteen Indians lay dead. Kit felt sick. He had never killed a man before. Young put his arm around the boy.

"Bad, isn't it?" he said. "But with a fighting Indian, it's him or you every time. Remember that, Kit."

Chapter 5

Little Chief of the Cheyennes

Ewing Young liked young Carson. He took Kit on a trip to California. It was almost the end of both of them. Crossing the desert, the entire party nearly died of thirst. They were also attacked by Indians. Kit Carson was going to a rough school.

On his return, Kit went trapping again in the Rockies. He went with famous mountain men like Jim Bridger.

Then he heard that Captain Bent was looking for men. Kit rode along the Arkansas River until he found him.

Captain Bent was glad to see his young friend. "How old are you now, lad?"

"Twenty-two," said Kit. Then he added sadly, "Haven't grown taller, just older."

"Is that your own horse?"

"Yes, sir. I bought him with money I made trapping beaver. His name is Squaw Man." Kit rubbed his horse's neck proudly.

"How would you like to work for me, lad?" asked Bent. "The Indians keep raiding my trading post, so I'm building a fort. I need a good man to take charge of the log-cutting crew."

Kit beamed. "I'd like that fine."

Kit lost no time setting up the logging camp. Captain Bent gave him a crew of strong men. The work went well.

One cold winter night two friendly Cheyenne Indians visited the camp. Their names were Little Turtle and Black Whiteman. When they tied up their ponies, they were surprised no one was guarding the horses. But they said nothing.

In the morning, only the two Indian ponies were left. All the other horses were gone.

During the night, 60 Crow Indians had crept into the camp. They stole all the horses. They did not want Indian ponies.

Kit Carson did not lose his temper easily. But now he was hopping mad. "Grab your blanket rolls, men," he yelled. "We're going after them."

The men thought Kit was out of his mind. "The Crows have a 20 mile lead," they said. "How can we catch them? We have to travel on foot."

Kit knew he ought to go back to the trading post for help. But he was ashamed to face Captain Bent. He was angry at himself for leaving the horses unguarded.

"We're going," he said stubbornly. "The Crows won't be looking for us. They left a clear trail. We can follow it easily. We *must* get back our horses!" Squaw Man was the only thing Kit owned, other than his father's gun.

Only a real leader could get men to go on such a hopeless chase. But the men followed Kit Carson. Black Whiteman and Little Turtle rode along beside them, laughing. They thought Kit was crazy.

For two full days, Kit and his men trudged northward. When they reached the Rockies, they ran into snow. The wind stung their faces. They plodded on without speaking. They did not want Indians to hear them.

Suddenly Kit pointed ahead. Smoke rose from a clump of pines. They had found what they were looking for.

"You two ride ahead and hide," Kit said to Little Turtle and Black Whiteman. "When we attack, you can get the horses."

The two friendly Indians nodded. By now, even they wanted to do what Kit Carson said.

Kit and his men crept quietly toward the Crow's camp.

"BOW-WOW-WOW-WOW — WOW-WOW!" A dog jumped out of the bushes. In a flash, the Crows came charging through the pine trees. They waved bows and arrows and scalping knives.

Kit remembered something he learned from Ewing Young. "Hide!" he yelled. "Hold your fire! Don't shoot till I tell you!"

Kit and his men ducked behind trees and bushes. The Indians thundered toward them. When Kit could almost touch their leader, he shouted, "FIRE!"

All the guns banged at once. Three Indians fell. The rest dashed toward the pines. Kit and his men ran after them.

The Crows raced after the horses. But the horses were gone! In a panic, the Crows fled. They thought a large force was after them.

Kit's men threw themselves on the ground. They were panting and sweating. Little Turtle and Black Whiteman rode up with the horses. The men cheered. They shook Kit's hand. Kit ran to get Squaw Man. Happily he rubbed his horse's nose.

The men rode the horses back to Bent's Trading Post. Little Turtle and Black Whiteman went back to the Cheyennes. They told everyone how Kit Carson had outfought the fierce Crows.

Yellow Wolf, chief of the Cheyennes, listened. Then he rode his pony to Bent's Fort.

"I wish to see the small white leader who chased the Crows," he told Bent.

Bent sent for Kit. All the other men gathered around.

"Small white man," commanded Yellow Wolf, "kneel down."

Kit was puzzled, but he did as he was told. The chief raised his hand above Kit's head.

"My son," he said, "you have a brave heart. You went after your horses on foot and got them back. With few men, you beat many Crows. From this day, among my people, your name will be *Vih'hui-nis,* Little Chief of the Cheyennes."

Chapter *6*

Saved by a Nose

Kit Carson was becoming famous throughout the Rockies. Now he no longer worked for others. He arranged his own expeditions. *He* was the leader. Many men wanted to sign up with him, but Kit would take only a few good men. No one could judge a trapper better than Kit Carson.

One summer Kit and his party trapped in the Medicine Bow Mountains.

They had good luck. But as winter came on, their food grew scarce. Kit started searching for game.

One afternoon he galloped into camp. "At last I found something," he said. "I saw signs of elk. I'm going to track the elk on foot."

Tom Cotton brought Kit's flintlock. "Want me to go with you?"

"No. It's better alone. Tonight we eat elk, Tom, or I'm a monkey's uncle."

Kit started off into the woods. "Don't let Uncle Grizzly get you," called Tom.

Kit's moccasins padded silently along the trail. He sniffed the air like a bloodhound. He knew Tom was not joking. This was grizzly bear country. No Indian would venture into grizzly country alone.

The grizzly bear is the most dangerous animal in the Rocky Mountains. He is also the strongest. A full-grown grizzly weighs more than one thousand pounds and is seven feet tall. His front paws, which he uses like hands, are a foot wide. He is clever, fearless and fierce.

But Kit Carson was not thinking about danger. His men needed food. He meant to get it for them, no matter what the risk. Like all real leaders, Kit Carson thought of his men first.

Kit followed the elk tracks for several miles. At last he found a herd of fat elk grazing on a hillside. Carefully, Kit crept into a clump of pines. Now the elk were in front of him. He raised his gun and fired. One buck staggered and fell. The others vanished.

Kit ran forward. Suddenly, he heard a roar behind him. He whirled around. Two huge grizzly bears were charging toward him.

Kit thought fast. His gun was empty. He could not reload now. He could see the bears' teeth flashing. He knew their sharp claws were ready to tear him to bits.

Kit had only one chance. He dropped his precious gun and ran. He ran as he had never run before.

In a short race a grizzly can outrun a race horse. But Kit was trying to outrun death. He streaked for cover. If only he could reach the trees! Kit pounded over the ground. The bears were hot behind him. He grabbed a branch and swung himself into a tree.

One bear stabbed at Kit with his big paw. It ripped off a moccasin. Kit scrambled up higher.

Bears climb trees and Kit knew it. He pulled out his hunting knife. He hacked off a short, thick branch to use as a club. "I don't think a bear can climb this small a tree," thought Kit, "but I can. Maybe it's lucky to be little."

The male grizzly was furious. He fumed and raged and foamed at the mouth. He backed away and charged the tree. His thousand pounds shook it like a hurricane. Kit hugged the tree. He held on.

Again and again the big bear beat against the tree. When it would not break, he began to bellow and snort.

He jerked small trees from the ground. He clawed at the roots of Kit's tree. Then he tried to climb up it. The trunk bent over. "This is the end," thought Kit.

The bear's paw raked Kit's drawn-up legs. Kit clutched the club he had cut. CRASH! He banged it down on the bear's nose. Crash! Crash! Crash! Kit clubbed the bear again and again.

The grizzly gave a scream of pain. He fell to the ground. He rolled over and over.

Kit was so weak he could hardly hang on to the tree. He leaned his head against the trunk and waited.

The bear picked himself up. He shook himself and joined his mate, who was eating the dead elk.

Kit clung to the tree. He thought, "I said we'd eat elk, or I'm a monkey's uncle. Guess I look like a monkey's uncle. I feel like one, too."

The moon rose and the wind moaned in the trees. Kit still did not move from his branch. It was midnight before he dared drop to the ground.

He picked up his gun and ran for camp. His men were huddled around the fire, waiting. They were afraid something had happened to him. They were right—something had. For the rest of his life, Kit called his escape from the grizzlies *my worst difficult experience*.

Chapter 7

Singing Grass

The trapping season ended after the beavers shed their winter coats. Then the trappers enjoyed themselves. In the summer of 1835, the trappers, traders and Indians held a great get-together in the Green River Valley. These get-togethers were the biggest event in a mountain man's year.

Their camp-out lasted as long as the hot weather. They enjoyed wrestling, horse racing, shooting and dancing.

There were lots of contests with the friendly Indians.

Kit Carson and his friend big Jim Bridger hurried to the Green River Valley to join the fun. They liked to visit the Arapaho Indians who were camped nearby. The Arapahos were the happiest of all tribes. They hated fighting and killing. They loved music and dancing and laughter, and they sang beautifully.

Every evening the Arapahos danced in a meadow by the river. One evening, Kit and Jim arrived at sunset. The dancing was going full tilt.

"Psst," whispered Jim, poking Kit, "I smell trouble." He pointed to a man watching the dancers. Kit recognized a giant French-Canadian called Shunar.

Shunar was a well-known bully. Wherever he went, he started a fight. He liked to find smaller men and beat them to a pulp. No one dared stand up to Shunar the Bully.

Shunar had been drinking firewater and was unsteady on his feet. His eyes were on one of the dancing girls. Kit followed the bully's gaze. The young Indian was beautiful. She wore a white buckskin dress trimmed with colored beads. Her smooth black hair shone in the firelight. Her skin was golden brown.

"You can't speak to an Arapaho girl without her father's permission," said Jim. "Look at that Shunar. He's going after her."

Shunar pushed through the dancers.

He knocked young braves right and left. He grabbed the beautiful Indian maiden and tried to kiss her. Quick as a flash, she slapped his face. She tore herself loose and raced lightly into the woods.

BOOM! BOOM! BOOM! Indian drums suddenly began beating war chants. Shunar stood in the middle of the ring, glaring. He looked like an angry ape.

"White bully touch Waa-nibe," thundered the chief. "Indian kill him." The braves began to close in on Shunar.

"WAIT!" Kit Carson held up his hand. He stalked up to the giant Shunar. "Lay your hands on another woman, Shunar, and I'll rip you to pieces."

Like all bullies, Shunar wanted to scare people. But he could see Kit was not afraid. Shunar ran. He grabbed his gun and jumped on his horse. Kit jumped on Squaw Man. He clutched his father's flintlock.

The two men charged at each other. ZOW! They both fired. Shunar's bullet ripped through Kit's hair. Kit's bullet hit Shunar's heart. The bully tumbled over, dead.

That night, Kit could not sleep. But he wasn't worrying about Shunar's death. Shunar had killed many good men. Like a mad dog, he had to be put away. Kit could not sleep because he was thinking about the Indian girl. "Waa-nibe means Singing Grass," Kit thought. "She is as lovely as her name."

Next day Waa-nibe's father sent for Kit. He wanted to thank him. Kit gazed at Waa-nibe. She gave him a shy smile. Kit's heart melted.

Not long afterward, Kit Carson and Waa-nibe were married. The Indian wedding took place in her father's wigwam. The chief spread his blanket over the shoulders of Waa-nibe and the "Little Chief of the Cheyennes." This meant Kit and Waa-nibe were now man and wife.

Chapter 8

The Pathfinder's Pathfinder

From his young Indian bride Kit learned many things. He began to understand the way Indians thought.

A baby girl was born to the young couple. Kit was happy because she looked like her beautiful mother. "We will call her Adaline," he said.

Waa-nibe nodded. Good Indian wives always agreed with their husbands.

Kit now had a new reason to go

trapping. "You and Adaline will stay at Bent's Fort," he said. "I'll trap the Blackfoot country."

"But the Blackfoot land is full of danger," said Waa-nibe.

"It's also full of beaver," said Kit. "I'll make a lot of money. Then we'll settle in Taos. We'll live quietly and raise a family."

Waa-nibe knew this was a dream. Kit Carson could never settle down. To tame him would be like putting an eagle in a birdcage.

Kit took 40 of his "Carson Men" with him on this trapping expedition. They were successful wherever they went.

One day a messenger came riding after Kit. He had some terrible news.

Waa-nibe was ill. She had prairie fever. To reach her, Kit rode Squaw Man 180 miles in two days. Kit rushed to Waa-nibe's bedside. His wife died in his arms.

Kit was heartbroken. Captain Charles Bent tried to comfort him. "Death is part of life, lad," he said.

"How will I take care of Adaline?" moaned Kit.

"The frontier is no place for a motherless girl," said Bent. "Have you relatives who could care for her?"

"I have a sister in Saint Louis," Kit muttered.

"You should take Adaline to her," said Captain Bent.

Kit did as the captain suggested. He hated to say good-by to his daughter.

But his sister loved the child at first sight. That made it easier.

On the riverboat returning from Saint Louis, Kit made a new friend. This friendship became important. It helped shape the history of the American West.

Kit was standing on deck when a stranger spoke to him. "I'm Charles Frémont," he said. "They tell me you're the famous Indian scout, Kit Carson."

"Not very famous," mumbled Kit.

"I'm going West to map the Oregon country for the government," Frémont said. "I'm going to need help. Are you interested?"

"I can't read or write," said Kit. "I don't own a compass or a watch. What help would I be?"

Frémont laughed. "I hear your mind *is* a map. They say you know every stream, canyon and mountain in the West. I want you to act as my guide. I'll pay you 100 dollars a month."

Thus began the famous friendship. With Kit as his guide, Frémont explored and mapped the Oregon Trail. Kit saved Frémont's life several times. Frémont was deeply grateful.

When his job was done, Kit hurried back to Taos to see Captain Charles Bent's sister-in-law, Josefa Jaramillo. He had fallen in love with her, although she was fifteen and he was 35. But young Josefa was both wise and beautiful. She and Kit were married in 1843.

Kit and Josefa had several children.

Still, Kit never really settled down. He took Frémont on two more expeditions. They brought back valuable maps and information about the West. They even found a way over the Sierra Mountains. It is still called Carson Pass.

John Charles Frémont became a famous man. He was called "The Pathfinder." But those who knew said that Kit Carson was "The Pathfinder's Pathfinder."

Chapter *9*

Adios

Kit Carson is remembered for his reckless bravery. Yet in his later years, his work among the Indians was just as remarkable.

In 1853 Kit was made Indian Agent in Taos. He held his job for seven years. He did great work helping the whites to understand the Indians. *"There were few bad Indians before the white man took away their means of gaining a living,"* Kit told the government.

"The Indian is starving. It is your responsibility to feed him."

When the Civil War began, Kit became a soldier. He was a colonel in the New Mexico Volunteers. He fought bravely, but he hated war. He was glad when the war ended.

Now Kit could go back to his work with the Indians. He worked hard for the Indian Treaty Commission. General John Pope said: *"Carson is the best man in the country to control these Indians. He is personally known and liked by every Indian of the bands likely to make trouble."*

But Kit's time was running out. His health was poor. He was hurt badly when he fell from a wild horse. When Josefa died, Kit's spirit was broken.

On May 23, 1868, after Josefa's death, Kit and a doctor friend sat talking. "Kit," the doctor teased, "they sure tamed the 'Pathfinder of the West.' You used to be as wild as a mustang."

Kit leaned back and closed his eyes. "Doc, it wasn't me that changed. It was my world. The mountains are covered with roads now. Even that railroad is coming out here. My world's gone, Doc."

The two men fell silent. The sun set. Kit lit up his pipe.

"Didn't I tell you not to smoke?" asked the doctor.

"Indeed you did." A twinkle came into Kit's tired eyes. "You told me to eat mush, too. But I just finished a big steak and a cup of black coffee."

Kit blew a cloud of smoke. "I'm not afraid of doctors or death—just grizzly bears!"

Doc laughed, but he was worried. No matter what he did, Kit's health grew worse. Everyone knew the end must be near.

Suddenly, Kit began coughing. He doubled up with pain. Doc bent over him, but there was nothing he could do. "I'm gone," Kit whispered. *"Adios, compadre.* Good-by, my friend."

With those words, Kit Carson died. And with him died the wild, uncharted West.

> *The rails were made,*
> *The wars were won,*
> *Ole Kit Carson,*
> *His job was done.*